# About The Che

Hello, my names John, I am a retired chef from the north east of England in the UK, and welcome to my first recipe book.

I'm a self taught chef that has been in the catering trade for over 35 years, since retiring I have found a new passion in sharing some of our favourite recipes on YouTube.

You can view every recipe in this book via video format on YouTube
at
www.youtube.com/user/jonboy2478

# Disclaimer Page

# Professional Food Homemade

Wonderful professional recipes from our commercial kitchens that you can make in your own home

By
John Kirkwood

# Acknowledgements

My first successful YouTube video of French baguettes was a total fluke, as I was just trying to show my friend Patrick, on how to make them in his own kitchen. I didn't know that the channel would be as popular as it is today, and that is due my fantastic viewers who have stuck by my side, and have tuned in for every new video recipe, for the last couple of years.

I would also like to thank the donators on both Patreon and PayPal, who have enabled me to buy new ingredients, and help with production costs. If it wasn't for you, the channels quality would have been significantly lower.

I would also like to thank my wife Terina and friend Harvey for all their support with this book.

# Contents

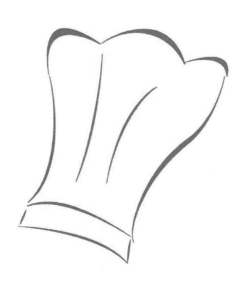

# Soft Sandwich Bread

## Ingredients

430g / 15.2 oz of Strong White Bread Flour
245g / 8½ oz of Warm Water 40°C / 104°F
20g / 1½ tbls of Vegetable or Olive oil
6g /1½tsp instant or active dried yeast
8g / 1tsp Table Salt
6g / 1tsp Sugar

Large Loaf/ 57% Hydration

## Method

**1.** Add the sugar, yeast and oil to the warm water, stir well and set it aside until the mixture starts to foam up (approx 10 minutes ) if your yeast has not activated by this time, then it must be dead, and needs replacing.

**2.** Mix the flour and salt together in a separate bowl.

**3.** Once your yeast has shown signs of life, add the yeast mixture to your stand mixer bowl, turn the machine on at its lowest setting with the dough hook attached, carefully spoon in the flour and salt mixture while the machine is running, allow the mixer to knead the dough for 10 minutes.

**4.** If you are kneading this dough by hand, add all of the ingredients to a bowl and partially mix everything together, turn it out onto your worktop, and knead the dough for 10 minutes, then carry on with the recipe below.

**5.** Turn out the dough from the mixer and form it into a ball, place it into a lightly oiled bowl coating the top of the dough too, cover the bowl and let it rise for at a minimum of 1 hour, the dough should at least double in size (this may take longer depending on the temperature in your kitchen).

**6.** In the meantime grease a 900g / 2lb loaf tin/pan, you can use, butter, lard, or shortening.

**7.** After the first rise, turn out the proven dough onto a lightly floured surface, knock the dough back for 1 minute, and form it into an fat sausage shape, place the dough into the prepared loaf tin/pan, sprinkle the dough with a little flour, cover it with a lightweight dry cloth, and set your timer for 1 hour or until it has risen 40mm / 1½in above the top of the tin, (once again this may take longer or shorter, depending on the temperature in your kitchen)

**8.** When there is about 10 minutes left on your second rise, preheat your oven to 180°C  355°F  gas mark 5

**9.** Once your dough has sufficiently risen, sprinkle a little more flour on the top, and place it in the middle of the preheated oven, and set your timer for 30 minutes.

**10.** Optional:  you can turn the loaf around in the oven after 20 minutes for even baking.

**11.** Carefully remove from the oven, pop it out of the tin and allow it to cool on a wire rack, for 30 minutes.

# Bloomer Loaf

## Ingredients

500g / 17½oz Strong white bread flour
310g / 11oz Water
45g / 3tbls Olive oil
2tsp / 7g Active or Instant dried yeast
8g /1tsp Salt

___

Large Loaf / 62% Hydration

## Method

**1.** Add the flour salt and yeast to a bowl and mix together with a whisk, (always make sure your yeast is healthy, before starting any bread recipe)

**2.** In a stand mixer, add the water and oil turn the machine on at its slowest setting with dough hook attached.

**3.** Spoon in the flour mixture gradually while the machine is running, allow the mixer to knead the dough for 10 minutes.

**4.** If you are kneading this dough by hand, add all of the ingredients to a bowl, partially mix it all together, tip it out onto your worktop and knead the dough for 10 minutes, then carry on with recipe below.

**5.** Turn out the dough from the mixer and form it into a ball, place it into a lightly oiled bowl, cover the bowl and let it rise for at a minimum of 1 hour, the dough should at least double in size (this may take longer, depending on the temperature in your kitchen).

**6.** Grease a large baking tray.

**7.** After the first rise, turn out the proven dough onto a lightly floured surface, knock the dough back for 1 minute, and form it into an oval shape, place the dough in the middle of your greased baking tray (see overleaf) sprinkle the dough with a little flour, cover it with a dry lightweight cloth and set your timer for 1 hour (once again this may take longer depending on the temperature in your kitchen).

**8.** When there is only 15 minutes left on your second rise, preheat your oven to 200°C / 390°F / gas mark 6, at the same time carefully place a pan of hot water on the bottom shelf of your oven (this creates a steamy atmosphere that makes the bread crispy) also have a spray bottle of water handy.

**9.** Once the dough has risen sprinkle a little more flour on the top of the now fully risen dough, and score the top of the bread 4 or 5 times with a very sharp knife of lame: (A lame is a curved bakes razor blade) place the loaf in the preheated oven (open the oven door slowly, to prevent a blast of steam) give the inside of the oven a quick spray with water, from a spray bottle, close the door and set your timer for 30 minutes, for a harder crust, bake for 40 to 45 minutes.

**10.** Optional: you can turn the loaf around in the oven after 20 minutes for even baking. Carefully remove from the oven and allow it to cool on a wire rack for 30 minutes.

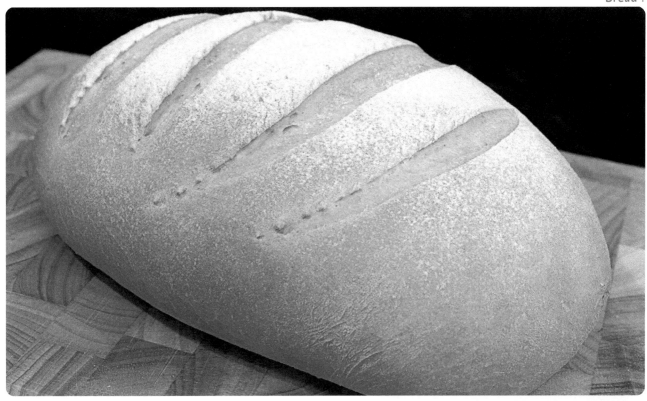

# Focaccia Bread

## Ingredients

600g / 21oz Strong white bread flour
360g / 12½oz Room temperature bottled or filtered water
7g / 2tsp instant or active dried yeast, fresh yeast 20g
1tsp / 8g Salt
***The Topping***
15g / ½oz Fresh Basil leaves
3 to 4 Garlic cloves
3½tbls / 50g Extra virgin olive oil
½tsp / 4g Salt
1½tbls Olive oil: to coat the bottom of the baking pan

Baking tin/pan, inside dimensions 12 x 8x 2in / 30 x 20 x 5cm

---

Serves 8 / 60% Hydration

## Method

**1.** Add the flour to a bowl, mix in the salt followed by the dried yeast, give these dry ingredients a thorough mix.
(always make sure your yeast is healthy, before starting any bread recipe)

**2.** Add the water and bring it all together into a slightly sticky dough, cover the bowl and allow it to rise for 45 minutes, this may take a little longer, depending on the temperature of your kitchen.

**3.** Once the dough has at least doubled in size, turn it out onto a slightly wet surface, and with very wet hands, give the dough a few turns for about 30 seconds, then get it back into the bowl, cover and set your timer for 30 minutes.

**4.** While waiting for the dough on this second rise, generously oil a baking pan with 1½ tablespoons of olive oil.
(see ingredient list: for baking pan size)

**5.** From the topping list, mince together the basil, garlic, salt and olive oil into a paste, You can do this in a pestle and mortar, or you can use a mini processor, once done, set it aside until needed.

**6.** Once the dough has at least doubled in size, turn it out onto a floured surface, add a little flour to the dough and shape into a rectangle using a rolling pin to the inside size of the baking pan/tin.

**7.** Place the dough rectangle in the oiled baking tin and stretch it out until it covers the bottom of the tin.

**8.** Spread the basil and garlic mixture all over the dough, and with your fingers, tamper it down until you achieve a dimple effect.

**9.** Loosely cover the dough with cling film / plastic wrap, place the tin in a draught free spot and set your timer for 45 minutes, once again this time may vary.

**10.** When there is only 10 minutes left on the rise time, preheat your oven to a pretty hot 220°C / 430°F / gas mark 7.

**11.** Once the dough has reached the top of the tin carefully and slowly peel back the cling film and get it into the preheated oven, and set your timer for 20 minutes, for even cooking you can turn the pan around at the halfway point.

**12.** Once the time is up, take it out of the oven and remove it from the baking pan using a couple of wire racks.

**13.** Once it's out of the tin and on the wire rack, drizzle a little more olive oil over the top while it's still hot, grate a little Parmesan cheese over, and it's ready to tear or cut, and serve.

# English Teacakes

## Ingredients

520G / 18½oz  Strong white bread flour
300g / 11oz  of lukewarm milk
1 Large egg (beaten)
40g /2½tbls / 1½oz Vegetable/Olive oil
60g / 2½oz Granulated sugar
7g / 2tsp / ¼oz dried yeast
150g / 5½oz mixed fruit and peel
Zest of 1 lemon
½tsp Salt
8g / 2tsp Ground allspice
1tsp ground Cinnamon
*Glaze ingredients*
30g hot water or Lemon juice
30g Sugar

---

Makes 8 / 67% Hydration

---

## Method

**1.** Start the recipe by adding the yeast and the sugar to the lukewarm milk, (approx 40°C / 104°F) mix thoroughly, set it aside until it foams up: between 5-10 minutes.

**2.** Meanwhile add the flour and the rest of the dry ingredients to a separate bowl, and mix thoroughly using a whisk.

**3.** To a stand mixer with the dough hook attached, add the proven yeast mixture, beaten egg, and oil, turn on the machine and gradually add the flour mixture.

**4.** Knead the dough on the slowest speed until it releases from the sides of the bowl, this could take anywhere from 10 to 15 minutes.

**5.** Turn out the dough onto a floured surface and form into a ball, place the dough ball into a lightly oiled bowl, coat the top of dough with a little oil, cover and allow it to rise for at least 1 hour, this time may vary, depending on the temperature of your kitchen.

**6.** After the 1 hour, the dough should have at least doubled in size, knock it back, and divide it into 8 equal pieces, form each piece into a ball shape, and leave them to rest for 10 minutes, this rest period will allow you to form the final shape much easier.

**7.** In the meantime grease 2 baking sheets with butter, lard or shortening.

**8.** After the 10 minute rest, form each ball into a disc shape, and place 4 on each of the greased trays. cover with a dry lightweight cloth, and allow them to rise for 1 hour, once again this may time may vary, depending on the temperature of your kitchen.

**9.** When there is only 10 minutes left on the rise time, preheat your oven to 190°C / 375°F /gas mark 5.

**10.** Place the risen teacakes in the oven and bake for 15-17 minutes.

**11.** Add 30g / 2tbls of sugar to a small container, add 30g / 2 tbls of hot water and mix until the sugar has dissolved.

**12.** Place the baked teacakes on a wire rack and brush with the glaze while they are still hot, allow to cool for 30 minutes.

**13.** These delicious teacakes are best, and traditionally served toasted, with lots of butter and or strawberry jam.

# Traditional French Baguettes

## Ingredients

700g / 25oz Strong white bread flour

520g/ mls / 19oz  Cold water

1tsp / 8g   Salt

½tsp / 2g   Dried yeast

If you are using fresh yeast:  8g

---

### Makes 4 Baguettes / 74% Hydration

---

## Method

**1.** Start the recipe by adding the flour, yeast, and salt to a bowl, mix these dry ingredients together, add the water and bring it all together to a sticky shaggy dough, see (Fig1) opposite.

**2.** Cover the bowl and set your timer for 45 minutes.

**3.** After the 45 minutes, turn the dough out onto a none floured wet surface, and with wet hands knock the dough back by giving it 5 or 6 turns. Repeat this procedure another 3 times, these very important 45 minute rest and rise periods give this style of bread its classic, and unique, texture and flavour.

**4.** After the last 45 minute rise, carefully turn out the dough onto a well floured surface, and divide it into 4 equal pieces, pre-shape the pieces as shown in (Fig2) opposite, cover them with a piece of oiled cling film / plastic wrap and let them rest for 15 minutes.

**5.** After the 15 minutes, form each piece into a baguette shape see (fig3) and transfer the baguettes to a couche cloth, (I use a white cotton pillowcase, see Fig4) cover with a dry lightweight cloth, and allow them to rise for 30 minutes.

**6.** When there is only 10 minutes left on the final rise, place a pan of hot water on the bottom shelf of your oven, and preheat your oven to 230°C  / 445°F, you will also need a spray bottle of water handy.

**7.** When the times up carefully transfer the baguettes, using a peel see (fig5) to 2 baking trays, 2 baguettes per tray, with a very sharp knife or bakers lame, carefully score the baguettes 4 times on each one, see (fig6).

**8.** Now carefully get them into the preheated oven, quickly, but carefully spray a little water in the oven and set your timer for between 16 and 20 minutes depending on how well done you prefer your baguettes.

**9.** When removing them, slowly open the oven door, so you don't get a blast of steam, remove them from the oven and onto a wire rack to cool.

---

### Bread making tips

---

**1.** Stick to the recipe rigidly, the quantities and ingredients are very important and carefully worked out for successful results.

**2.** Try to use digital scales for all of the measurements including the water,  converting to cups and measuring jugs is fine, but weighing the ingredients is much more accurate, the gram is my unit of choice.

**3.** Use proper bread flour with at least 12% protein, check the ingredients list on the side of the flour bag for the protein level, protein may show in grams per serving but just work it out, it needs to be 12g of protein per 100g of flour. Plain or all purpose flour has a lower protein count and is great for pastries, cakes, and biscuits, but is NOT strong enough for making bread.

**4.** Very important...Check your yeast is working, BEFORE you start any bread recipe.

Fig 1

Fig 2

Fig 3

Fig 4

Fig 5

Fig 6

# Hot Dog Buns
## No Knead Recipe

## Ingredients

560g / 20oz Strong white bread flour
200g / 7oz Full or half fat milk
(Lukewarm 40°C / 104 F°)
120g / 4oz Water (Lukewarm 40°C / 104 F°)
1 Large egg
20g/⅓oz/1⅓tbls Vegetable or olive oil
20g Sugar
8g / 1tsp Salt
7g / 2tsp Instant or active dried yeast, if using fresh yeast; 20g/ ⅓oz

Makes 8 / 64% Hydration

## Method

**1.** Start by adding the milk,water, beaten egg, sugar, and yeast, to a jug and allow the warm liquid to proof for 5 to 10 minutes.

**2.** In a large bowl, add the flour and mix in the salt using a whisk.

**3.** Add the warm proven yeast mixture to the flour, followed by the oil, mix the ingredients until you have everything combined into a sticky dough.

**4.** Cover the bowl and set your timer for 1 hour, (proofing times may vary depending on the temperature of your kitchen).

**5.** Grease a large baking tray, ideal tray size, 14 x 9in / 35 x 24cm.

**6.** After 1 hour, the dough should have at least doubled in size, turn it out onto a floured surface, lightly flour the dough, and knead for 1 minute.

**7.** Divide the dough into 8 equal pieces, and form them first into a ball, then a short sausage shape, and let them relax for 1 minute, .

**8.** Next form them into a medium sausage shape, and let those relax for one minute, (these short rest periods, makes the dough much easier to shape).

**9.** For the final shaping, form them into the finished shape (approx 15cm / 6in long) and place them onto the greased baking tray, dust with a little flour, cover them with a dry lightweight cloth and allow them to rise for 45 minutes, (proofing times may vary depending on the temperature of your kitchen).

**10.** When there is 10 minutes left on the final rise, preheat your oven to 180°C / 355°F / gas mark 4.

**11.** When the buns have sufficiently risen, place the tray in the centre of the  preheated oven, and bake for 16 minutes, the tray can be turned halfway through, for even cooking.

**12.** Remove from the oven, and off the tray onto a wire rack, and allow them to cool for 30 minutes.

# Pita Bread

## Ingredients

375g / 13oz Plain or all purpose flour
240g / 240mls / 8½oz Lukewarm water: approx 40°C / 104°F
7g / 2tsp instant dried yeast
15g / 1 tbls Olive oil
15g / 1tbls Sugar
8g / 1tsp Salt

Makes 8 / 64% Hydration

## Method

**1.** Add all of the ingredients to a bowl or stand mixer.

**2.** If you are using a stand mixer use the dough hook attachment, and mix for 10 minutes.

**3.** If you making the dough by hand, knead this wet dough for 4 minutes, until it comes together (this is a very sticky dough, but do not add any extra flour), then knead for a further 6 minutes until it smooth and supple.

**4.** Place the processed dough in a lightly greased bowl, cover and allow it prove for at least 45 minutes, this time may vary depending on the temperature of your kitchen.

**5.** After the first proof, divide the dough into 8 pieces, roll each piece into a ball and allow the balls to rest for 10 minutes (this 10 minute rest period will make it much easier to form the final shape}.

**6.** After the 10 minute rest, roll out the dough balls into 15cm / 6" circles and place onto parchment lined baking trays, cover with a dry lightweight cloth, and rest them for 30 minutes

**7.** When there is only 10 minutes left on the timer, preheat a skillet or hot plate to a temperature of 300°C that's 570°F (Do not add any oils or fats, they will just burn).

**8.** Place each raw pita onto the hot dry skillet, and cook for 30 seconds on one side, flip it over and cook for a further 2 to 3 minutes or until thc pita blows up like a balloon and starts to colour.

**9.** Remove from the skillet onto a warm plate, continue until all 8 pita breads are cooked.

**10.** Fill with your favourite filling.

**11.** (Seepage 52-53) for my Dona kebab Meat recipe.

# Easy Egg Custard

## Ingredients

300mls milk (full or half fat)
300mls Double or heavy cream
5 Egg yolks
70g / 2½oz Granulated sugar
2tsp / 12g Vanilla extract
½tsp Corn flour / starch

Serves 6

## Method

**1.** Start the recipe by separating 5 (room temperature) egg yolks.

**2.** Heat the milk, vanilla extract, and cream in a suitable saucepan on a low to medium heat, bring to a simmer.

**3.** Meanwhile whisk the egg yolks and sugar until the colour turns a pale yellow, this takes approx 1 minute.

**4.** Add the corn flour/starch to the egg mixture and whisk in.

**5.** Pour 2 ladles of the hot milk/cream from the saucepan onto the egg mixture, and quickly whisk it in, this is to temper the eggs.

**6.** Now add the egg mixture, to the rest of the liquid in the saucepan, and very slowly bring it back to a simmer on a low heat.
Once the custard thickens it is ready to serve.

20

# Apple & Blackberry Crumble

## Ingredients

**Crumble mix**
200g / 7oz Plain / all purpose flour
125g / 4½oz Butter
125g / 4½oz Demerara or white sugar
50g / 2oz oats / Oatmeal ½tsp / 2g
Ground Cinnamon
½tsp / 2g Ground Nutmeg
**Filling**
1kg / 2¼lb Apples of your choice
140g / 5oz Blackberries
1 lemon zest and juiced
50g / 2oz Butter
50g / 2oz Granulated sugar
½tsp / 2g Ground Cinnamon

Serves 8

## Method

**1.** Start the recipe by finely grating the zest, and juicing 1 medium size lemon.

**2.** Wash, peel, core, and dice the apples into about ½in /13mm pieces, once all the apples are diced, coat them with lemon juice, to stop them from browning, and set them aside for now.

**3.** Making the crumble mix, add the flour, Sugar, Oats, spices and butter to a bowl and slowly start to rub the ingredients together with your finger, until you have a dry, course breadcrumb like consistency, once the crumble is made set it aside until needed.

**4.** Preheat your oven to 180°C / 355°F / gas mark 4.

**5.** Add the sugar from the filling ingredients list to a large hot frying pan or wok, when it dissolves and starts to turn brown carefully add the apples, cook and stir the apples for a couple of minutes, add the lemon zest and Cinnamon and mix in, finally add the butter, stir and cook for 3 minutes

**6.** Transfer the cooked, hot apples to a suitable roasting pan or ceramic dish (Baking pan/dish, recommended size is 12 x 8 x 2in / 30 x 20 x 5cm ) spread the blackberries evenly across the apples, and completely and evenly cover the fruit with the crumble mix .

**7.** Get it into the preheated oven and set your timer for 30 minutes.

**8.** Once the time's up, take it out, and let it relax for a moment, serve hot or cold with custard or vanilla ice cream.

**9.** See page 21. How to make Egg Custard.

# Jam & Sponge Pudding

## Ingredients

170g / 6oz  Jam of your choice

170g / 6oz Self raising flour, If using plain or all purpose flour, add an extra 8g / 2tsp Baking powder

85g / 3oz Granulated sugar

150g / 5½oz Vegetable or Sunflower oil

3 Large eggs

5g / 1tsp Baking powder

2g / ½tsp Salt

6g / 1tsp Vanilla extract

Serves 4-6

## Method

**1.** Grease and flour, a suitable pudding bowl, the sizes of the bowl for this recipe are 5½ x 3½ x 3in / 14 x 9 x 8cm, and place the jam in the bottom of the bowl, now place the bowl in the freezer for 30 minutes, to harden up the jam.

**2.** Before mixing the batter, preheat your oven to 170°C / 340°F gas mark 4.

**3.** Mix together the oil, eggs, vanilla extract, and sugar.

**4.** Sift in the flour, salt, and baking powder, push any lumps through with your fingers.

**5.** Mix the batter until smooth, you can use a stand or hand mixer to do this step.

**6.** Carefully pour the batter into the prepared bowl, without getting any on the sides of the bowl.

**7.** Give the bowl a couple of gentle taps on the bench to remove any large air bubbles.

**8.** Place the bowl on a baking tray, and get it into the preheated oven, set your timer for 50 minutes.

**9.** When the time is up check with a cocktail stick, if it comes out clean, it's done, if not give it another 5 minutes.

**10.** Once done, with oven mitts on, place the bowl upside down on a serving plate, give it a little shake, and lift the bowl vertically, and the pudding should slide out, and the jam, will cascade down over the pudding.

**11.** Scrape out any jam that may be stuck in the bowl.

**12.** Serve hot straight away with hot custard.

**13.** See page 21. How to make Egg Custard.

# Strawberry Pancakes

## Ingredients

250g / 9oz Plain or all purpose flour
300mls / 300g Milk
45g /3tbls Vegetable oil or melted butter
1 Large egg
3tsp / 15g Baking powder
1 tsp Vanilla extract
2g / ⅓tsp Salt
250g / 9oz Fresh Strawberries
30g / 1oz Granulated sugar
Butter and oil for frying
Maple syrup or honey

Serves 4-6

## Method

**1.** Start by washing/hulling/cutting the strawberries into small pieces.

**2.** In a small bowl add the sugar with the strawberries and mix until the sugar has completely dissolved, set it aside to macerate for 10 minutes.

**3.** In a large bowl, add the flour and salt; sift in the baking powder to remove any lumps, add the egg, milk, oil or melted butter, and vanilla extract, mix to a smooth lump free batter.

**4.** Heat up a large frying pan on a medium heat, add a little of the butter and oil combination

**5.** Ladle in as much or as little of the batter to suit the size of the pancakes you require, fry for 2 to 3 minutes on either side.

**6.** Stack the pancakes on a warm plate with the strawberry filling in between each pancake approximately 3 to 4 high.

**7.** Top the stack off with more of the strawberries, Drizzle with butter and honey or maple syrup, serve hot.

# Apple Pie

## Ingredients

### Pie Filling
1.4kg / 3lb Apples (Peeled chopped)
⅓ Lemon (juiced)
40g / 1½oz Brown sugar
40g / 1½oz butter
2tsp / 8g Corn flour / starch
1tsp / 4g Ground Cinnamon
½tsp / 2g Ground Nutmeg
1 Small egg (wash)
1tsp Granulated sugar (dusting)

### Pastry
300g / 10½oz Plain / All purpose flour
150g / 5½oz Cold butter (cubed)
100g / 2½oz Cold water
40g / 1½oz Granulated sugar
½tsp Salt

---

### Serves 8

## Method

**1.** Grease a 23x4cm / 9x1½in pie dish, with lard or butter and juice half a lemon.

**2.** Wash, peel, and chop the apples of your choice into chunks, coat the apple pieces in the lemon juice to prevent browning, add the Cinnamon, Nutmeg and Brown sugar to the apples, mix and cover the bowl with plastic wrap / cling film, and set it aside for at least 1 hour allowing the juice to seep out of the apples.

**3.** Time to make the pastry, you can make the pastry by hand or it is always best to use a food processor, put the flour, cold butter, sugar, and salt into the food processor and pulse for a few seconds until the ingredients resemble fine bread crumbs, next with the machine running, pour in the cold water until the pastry comes together (approx 45 seconds) don't over mix. Remove it from the machine divide it into 2 equal pieces, wrap each piece in cling film and refrigerate for 30 minutes.

**4.** Back to the apples, after an hour, pour the apples into a strainer so the juice runs into a separate bowl, once it has drained through, pour the juice into a microwavable container, add the butter from the filling ingredients list and microwave on full power for 30 seconds, mix the cornflour into the 40mls of cold water and add it to the juice, microwave once more in 30 sec intervals until the mixture thickens, then add the thickened juice back to the apples, and mix it all together, and that is the filling done.

**5.** At this point preheat your oven to 200°C / 390°F / Gas mark 6

**6.** Roll out the bottom pastry, and line the greased pie dish with it, add the apple filling, brush water around the edge of the pastry before adding the top pastry, gently press down around the edge with the palm of your hands, trim off the excess pastry, crimp the edges of the pie together, brush beaten egg over the whole surface, sprinkle with sugar, white or brown, cut a few vent holes, and get it into the preheated oven and set the timer for 45 minutes,

**7.** In the unlikely event of any leakage while baking, place a baking tray under the pie dish in the oven.

**8.** When the times up get the pie onto a wire rack and let it relax and settle for 20 to 30 minutes, slice and serve with vanilla ice cream, or custard.

**9.** See page 21. How to make Egg Custard.

# Custard Tart

## Ingredients

### Pastry
250g Plain or all purpose flour
130g Cold butter
60g/2oz Sugar
1 Egg (beaten)
20g/mls Milk
2g/½tsp Salt

### Custard
260mls Milk
260mls Double/heavy cream
100g Sugar
7 Egg yolks
10mls/2 tsp Vanilla extract
2g/½tsp Freshly grated nutmeg

Serves 8

## Method

**1.** Making the pastry, first beat the egg and the milk together, you can make this pastry by hand, or it's much better to use a food processor, put the flour, cold butter, sugar, and salt into the food processor and pulse for a few seconds until the ingredients resemble fine bread crumbs, next with the machine running, pour in the beaten egg and milk mixture until the pastry comes together (approx 45 seconds) do not over mix. Remove it from the machine, roll it into a flat disc, wrap it in cling film, and refrigerate for 30 minutes.

**2.** Preheat your oven to 180°C / 355°F / gas mark 4

**3.** Roll out the pastry, big enough to overlap a 20cm / 8in tart tin with a removable bottom.

**4.** Once the pastry is in the tin, (do not trim off the excess pastry), prick all over the bottom of the pastry with a fork, line the pastry with crumpled up parchment paper and blind bake it (using baking beans, uncooked rice or lentils is a good alternative) in the preheated oven for 20 minutes, after the 20 minutes remove the beans and paper, carefully trim off the excess pastry, brush with beaten egg to seal the pastry, and bake for a further 20 minutes.

**5.** In a bowl, separate 7 egg yolks, add the sugar and whisk until a light shade of cream.

**6.** Bring the cream, milk, and vanilla extract to a simmer in a suitable saucepan.

**7.** Carefully pour 2 ladles of the hot milk/cream from the saucepan onto the egg yolks and quickly whisk it in, this is to temper the eggs, once mixed in, slowly add the rest of the mixture to the yolks, and blend it all together, transfer it to a suitable jug, but pour the custard into a jug, through a fine sieve (this will get rid of most of the air bubbles)

**8.** Adjust your oven setting to 150°C / 300°F /gas mark 2 to 3.

**9.** Pour the custard into the pastry case to the top, grate some fresh nutmeg over the whole surface, and carefully get it into the preheated oven for 40 minutes.

**10.** Remove from the oven, allow to cool, slice a serve with whipped cream.

# Victoria Sponge

## Ingredients

### The Sponge
200g / 7 oz softened Butter (room temperature)
200g / 7oz Caster Sugar
250g / 9oz Self Raising Flour / if you use All Purpose or Plain Flour, add an extra 2 tsps of baking powder
5 Medium or 4 Large Eggs (roomtemperature)
2tsp Baking Powder
½tsp Vanilla Extract

### The Filling
300mls of double or heavy Cream
1½tsp Icing or Powdered Sugar
1tsp Vanilla Extract
120g of Jam
Powdered / Icing Sugar for dusting

---

Serves 8

---

## Method

**1.** Begin the recipe by preheating your oven to 190°C / 374°F Gas mark 5.

**2.** Grease two 20cm / 8" sandwich cake tins, and line the bottoms with greaseproof paper.

**3.** Add the butter and caster sugar to a bowl and cream together to a smooth paste, using a spatula.

**4.** Whisk in the eggs 1 at a time (make sure your eggs are at room temperature). Add the vanilla extract and mix in.

**5.** Sift in the flour and baking powder, and gently fold it into batter using a spatula.

**6.** Divide the batter equally into the 2 cake tins, and get them into the preheated oven, and set your timer for 23 minutes.

**7.** While the sponge is baking, start the Chantilly cream, by adding the double or heavy whipping cream, vanilla extract and icing sugar to a bowl, and whisk until medium soft peaks, refrigerate until needed.

**8.** Check the cakes after the 23 minutes ( do not open the oven door before) use a cocktail stick to test in the cake is done, if it comes out clean the cake is done, if not give it a couple of more minutes.

**9.** Place the tins on a wire rack for 10 minutes before removing the cakes from the tins, after the 10 minutes, remove from the tins and gently peel off the paper and allow to properly cool for a further 10 minutes.

**10.** Place one of the cakes on a serving plate (top down) with the flat bottom of the sponge facing up, cover with the jam of your choice staying shy of the edge, next cover the jam with the prepared Chantilly cream, gently line up and place the second cake on top of the cream with the flat bottom of the sponge facing down this time, gently press it down.

**11.** Finally dust with powdered / icing sugar, slice and serve.

32

# Lemon Drizzle Cake

## Ingredients

### The Cake
200g / 7oz Self raising flour, If using plain or all purpose flour, add extra 2tsp baking powder
110g / 4oz Granulated sugar
200g / 7oz Vegetable or Sunflower oil
4 Large eggs
Zest & Juice of 1 large or 2 small lemons
1tsp Baking powder
1tsp Vanilla extract
½tsp Salt

### Lemon Icing/frosting
100g 3½oz Icing/powdered sugar
2tbls Lemon Juice

Serves 6

## Method

**1.** First, grease and flour a 2lb / 900g loaf tin/pan, and Preheat your oven to 170°C / 340°F / Gas mark 4.

**2.** To a large bowl add the eggs, vanilla, lemon zest, sugar, and oil, and whisk for 1 minute.

**3.** Sift in the flour, baking powder, and salt, and whisk it in, until the batter is smooth.

**4.** Carefully pour the batter into the prepared loaf tin. place the tin in the middle of the oven and set the timer for 50 minutes.

**5.** While waiting for the cake to bake, add approx 2tbls of lemon juice to the icing/powdered sugar and mix until smooth.

**6.** In a separate small bowl, mix 3tbls/45mls of lemon juice, with 3tsp/20g of granulated sugar.

**7.** After the 50 minutes, check the cake is done by inserting a cocktail stick into the centre of the cake, if it comes out clean, the cake is done, if not give it a further 5 minutes.

**8.** Place the tin on a wire rack for 10 minutes to rest before removing it from the tin.

**9.** Turn out the cake from the tin, the cake should release quite easily.

**10.** Pierce a few holes in the top of the cake with a wooden skewer, and pour over the lemon juice and sugar mixture, until it all soaks into the sponge.

**11.** Now pour over the white lemon drizzle mixture, and let it flow and drizzle down the sides of the cake.

# Oatmeal & Chocolate Chip Cookies

## Ingredients

70g / 2½oz brown sugar
100g / 3½oz White granulated sugar
112g / 4oz Butter (room temperature)
6g /1tsp Vanilla extract
1 Large egg
130g / 4½oz Plain or all purpose flour
180g / 6½oz Rolled or instant oats
2g / ½tsp Salt
4g / 1tsp Baking powder
60g / 2oz White chocolate chips
60g / 2oz Dark or milk chocolate chips
20g / 1tble Honey
*Topping:*
100g / 3½oz white chocolate
30g / 1oz Cocoa powder

Makes 12

## Method

**1.** Line two baking trays with parchment paper, and preheat your oven to 190°C / 375F or gas mark 5.

**2.** Start the recipe by adding both sugars and butter (make sure your butter is at room temperature) to the bowl, and cream those together, until you have a nice smooth paste.

**3.** Add the vanilla extract and egg, (once again make sure your egg is at room temperature), now mix until you have a smooth batter.

**4.** Next add all of the other dry ingredients, also the honey, mix it all together until you have sticky mass of cookie dough.

**5.** Divide the dough into 12 equal pieces, using digital scales, and roll each piece into a ball, then slightly flatten it.

**6.** Place the raw cookies on the prepared baking tray, equally spaced apart.

**7.** Place the cookies in the oven and set your timer for 13 minutes.

**8.** After the time is up place the trays on wire racks for 10 minutes.

**9.** After the 10 minutes remove them from the trays and paper, let them sit on the wire racks until completely cool.

**10.** You can have them as they are, or decorate them as shown in the image, by coating them with melted white chocolate, and using coffee stencils and cocoa powder, for the designs.

# Chocolate Muffins

## Ingredients

110g / 4oz Unsalted butter (room temperature)
150g / 5oz Castor sugar
3 medium size eggs, approx 150g / 5oz without the shell (beaten, room temperature)
110g / mls / 4oz full fat milk
180g / 6.½oz Self Raising flour, if using plain or all purpose flour add an extra 2tsp of baking powder
35g / 1.2oz Cocoa powder
4g /1tsp Baking powder
100g / 3½oz plain chocolate chips + plus extra for topping

### Makes 12 Medium size Muffins

## Method

**1.** Before starting the recipe, prepare a 12 cup muffin tin, by lining each cup with a medium size paper cake case, and preheat your oven to 180°C / 355°F or gas mark 4.

**2.** Cream the butter and the sugar together until soft, smooth and light, the colour should be a creamy white.

**3.** Add the beaten eggs in 3 to 4 stages.

**4.** Sift the flour, cocoa, and baking powders, into a separate bowl to get rid of any lumps.

**5.** Add half of the dry ingredients and milk to the mixture, and gently fold it in, once creamy, add the other half of the dry mixture and milk, and fold that in until you have a smooth creamy batter.

**6.** Add the chocolate chips and gently fold those in.

**7.** Divide the batter between the 12 muffin cases.

**8.** Sprinkle a few chocolate chips to the top of each muffin case, not too many, approx 8 or 9 to each muffin.

**9.** Place the tin into the preheated oven, and bake for 25 minutes.

**10.** When the time is up, test with a cocktail stick, if it comes out clean they are done, if not bake for a further 2 to 3 minutes.

**11.** Remove from the oven and allow to cool on a wire rack for at least 30 minutes.

# Jam & Coconut Cake

## Ingredients

175g / 6½oz Self raising flour, If using plain or all purpose flour add extra 2tsp baking powder
120g / 4½oz Granulated sugar
175g / 6½oz Vegetable or Sunflower oil
4 Large eggs
30g / 1oz Desiccated coconut
1tsp Baking powder
1tsp Vanilla extract
½tsp Salt
Jam and extra Coconut for topping

Serves 6

## Method

**1.** First job, grease and flour a 2lb / 900g loaf tin/pan, Preheat your oven to 170°C / 340°F / Gas mark 4.

**2.** To a large bowl add the eggs, vanilla extract, Coconut, sugar, and oil and whisk for 1 minute.

**3.** Sift in the flour, baking powder, salt, and whisk it in until the batter is smooth.

**4.** Carefully pour the batter into the prepared loaf tin.

**5.** Place the tin in the middle of the oven, and set the timer for 50 minutes.

**6.** After the 50 minutes check the cake is done by inserting a cocktail stick into the centre of the cake, if it comes out clean the cake is done, if not, give it a further 5 minutes.

**7.** Place the tin on a wire rack for 10 minutes before removing the cake from the tin.

**8.** Turn out the cake from the tin, cover the top with a jam of your choice, and sprinkle with more coconut.

**9.** Serve hot or cold, on it's own or with custard.

# Salmon & Broccoli Quiche

## Ingredients

### The Pastry
150g / 5½oz Plain or all purpose flour
50g / mls / Cold water
75g / 2½oz Cold butter
½tsp / 4g Table salt

### The Filling
4 Large eggs
150g / mls / 10½oz Single cream
50g / mls Milk full or half fat
½tsp Salt
½tsp Ground black pepper
175g / 6oz Tinned or fresh skinless and boneless salmon
100g / 3½oz Broccoli florets
60g / 2oz Mature grated cheddar cheese

Serves 6-8

## Method

**1.** To start the recipe, add the flour, salt, and cold butter to a food processor, and pulse it until it looks like fine breadcrumbs. If you are using your hands: rub the ingredients together as quickly as possible to prevent the butter melting.

**2.** Add the cold water and let the machine run until the pastry comes together in a ball, this should take no more than 45 seconds, by hand add the water and bring it together with an ordinary dinner knife, then knead the dough by hand, until it forms into a ball, always working quickly.

**3.** Roll the finished pastry into a ball flatten to form a disc, wrap it in cling film, and get into the fridge for at least 30 minutes, this can be done well in advance, even the day before.

**4.** Add the eggs, cream, milk, salt and pepper to a bowl and whisk for 1 minute.

**5.** Grease two 20cm/8in sandwich cake tin, with butter, lard, or shortening.

**6.** Roll out the chilled pastry to about an eighth of an inch or 3mm thick, and line the greased tin, make sure the pastry is gently tucked down into the corners of the tin, trim off the excess pastry, and with a fork, prick a few holes in the base of the pastry, this will stop it pushing up during baking.

**7.** Time to preheat your oven to 170°C / 340°F / gas mark 4.

**8.** Open the tin and drain the Salmon, then break it up into small flakes, break the broccoli up into small florets.

**9.** Putting it together, Spread half of the cheese over the bottom of the pastry, equally space out the salmon and broccoli florets, pour over the egg mixture, staying short of the top of the pastry, sprinkle over the rest of the cheese, and get it into the preheated oven for 50 minutes, you can turn the quiche around after 25 minutes for even cooking and rise.

**10.** After the time is up take it out of the oven, and allow it to completely cool on a wire rack, before removing it from the tin.

# Egg Fried Rice

## Ingredients

400g / 14oz Day old cooked Basmati rice
170 / 6oz King Prawns
1 Large egg
40g / 1½oz Frozen sweet peas
2 Spring/green onions finely chopped
4 baby carrots finely chopped
1 clove of garlic finely chopped
1 tsp Dark soy sauce
1 tsp Chicken or MSG granules
½ tsp Salt
*The rice ingredients: for 2 servings*
150g / 5½oz Basmati rice
1tsp Olive oil
½tsp Salt

Serves 2

## Method

**1.** Cook 150g / 5oz of basmati rice, the day before making the dish, by boiling it for for 8 minutes, drain and refrigerate overnight, as freshly cooked rice on the day would be too sloppy to make the fried rice.

**2.** Finely dice the onions, carrots and garlic and set aside, beat the egg.

**3.** If using raw prawns, pre part cook them in hot oil for 45 seconds.

**4.** Heat up your wok or frying pan (hot) and add 1tbls of vegetable oil and quickly cook the egg to a scrambled consistency, once cooked remove from the wok/pan, and set it aside.

**5.** Add another 1tbls of vegetable oil, and fry off the onions, garlic, and carrots for one minute.

**6.** Add the rice and break up any clumps, so it is all loose and single grained.

**7.** Add the seasoning, chicken powder or MSG, salt, and finally the soy sauce, mix and toss well for 2 minutes.

**8.** Add the egg back into the pan, mix again for one minute before adding the frozen peas.

**9.** Finally add the prawns, mix for a further minute until everything is piping hot and serve.

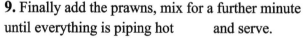

# Shepherds Pie

## Ingredients

1KG / 2.2LB Minced/Ground Lamb or Beef
1½kg / 3lb Potatoes
80g / 3oz Cheddar cheese (Grated)
100g / 3½oz Butter
1 Medium size onion
1 Large carrot
Small turnip or Swede
4g /1tsp Dried thyme
4g / ½tsp Salt
4g / ½tsp Salt for the potato water
15g / 1Tbls Vegetable oil
3 Stock cubes (optional)

Serves 6-8

## Method

**1.** Wash and peel the potatoes, and the other vegetables, cut the potatoes into equal size pieces, not too big, cover them in water in a pan, add the salt, bring them to a boil, turn the heat to medium, cover the pan, and let them boil for 20 minutes.

**2.** Meanwhile, dice the carrots and turnip into small pieces (approx 8mm cubes), and roughly chop the onions.

**3.** After the potatoes have been boiling for 10 minutes, in a large pan, fry off the onions in 1tbls of vegetable oil, until soft, add the minced/ground lamb or beef, and stir until hot, breaking up the meat.

**4.** Add the thyme, salt, and stock cubes then keep stirring until the meat has separated and loose, and brown in colour, (do not add any liquid).

**5.** Add the diced carrots and turnip to the meat, stir until hot again, cover the pan and let in sit on a low heat for 10 minutes.

**6.** After the potatoes have been boiling for 20 minutes, drain and mash them with the butter, and set it aside for now.

**7.** Time to preheat your oven to 200°C that's 390°F or gas mark 6

**8.** The meat and vegetables should be ready by this time, carefully scrape it all into a baking tin/pan, and level it off.  (Baking pan/tin dimensions are, 12 x 8 x 2in /30 x 21 x 5cm  )

**9.** Gently spoon the mashed potatoes onto the top of the meat, and carefully spread and level it out using a fork, you can create a line pattern in the potato with the fork, sprinkle the grated cheese over the mashed potatoes, add a little freshly ground pepper and sea salt.

**11.** Bake in the preheated for 15 minutes.

**12.** Remove from oven, serve hot straight from the tin.

# Cheese Scones

## Ingredients

225g / 8oz self raising flour
55g / 2oz Cold butter
100g / 3½oz Mature cheddar cheese
90g / mls / 3.2oz Milk
4g / 1 tsp baking powder
2g / ½tsp Mustard powder
1g / ½tsp Cayenne pepper
1g / ½tsp Turmeric
2g / ½tsp Salt
Extra cheese for topping
Milk for glazing

Makes 6

## Method

**1.** Before starting the recipe preheat your oven to 200°C / 390°F / gas mark 6.

**2.** Sift all of the dry ingredients into a bowl, add the cold butter, and rub together until it resembles fine bread crumbs.

**3.** Fold in the cheese with your fingers until it is evenly incorporated, add the milk and cut it in using a dinner knife.

**4.** Gently fold the mixture together into a dough by hand, taking care not to over handle the dough.

**5.** Roll the dough into a rectangle, approximately 25mm / 1 inch thick.

**6.** Cut the dough into 6 scones, using a 6cm scone cutter, if you don't have a scone cutter, just cut it into 6 equal squares with a knife.

**7.** Place the scones on a greased baking tray, brush the tops with milk, and add a little finely grated cheese to each one.

**8.** Place the tray into the preheated oven, and set your timer for 14 minutes, times may vary between 13 and 17 minutes, due to varying temperatures of different ovens.

**9.** When the time is up, remove them from the oven, they should be golden brown, allow them to completely cool on a wire rack.

**10.** Serve with plenty of butter.

# Yorkshire Puddings

## Ingredients

225g / 8oz Plain or All purpose flour
4 Large Eggs
148g / mls / ½pint water
148g / mls / ½pint milk
½tsp salt
85g / 3oz Beef dripping or Lard

Makes 12

## Method

**1.** Preheat the oven to 200°C / 390 / gas mark 6.

**2.** You'll need a 12 cup muffin tin, with 8g / ¼oz of beef dripping, lard, or vegetable oil, in each cup, place the tin in the middle of the oven at the start, to get it really hot.

**3.** Start the recipe by adding the eggs and salt to a bowl, and give those a good whisk until smooth, you can use a stand or a hand mixer to do this recipe.

**4.** Add the flour, and whisk until you have a smooth, thick, lump free paste.

**5.** Next, combine the milk and water in a separate jug, and add a little of the liquid to the paste, to loosen it up,(If you add all of the liquid at once it will become very lumpy) once you have a smooth, lump free batter, add the rest of the liquid and whisk or beat for 1 minute to incorporate plenty of air into the batter.

**6.** Transfer the batter from the bowl to a suitable jug; this will make it much easier to pour into the muffin tin cups.

**7.** Very carefully take the smoking hot tin out of the oven, and place it on a heat proof surface, (top of your stove is ideal) half fill each cup with the batter, if there is any left in the jug: share it out equally across the cups, get the tin back into the oven, and set your time for 30 minutes. (Do not open the oven door half way through, as the sudden drop in temperature will cause the puddings to collapse)

**8.** Once the time is up remove from the oven and serve straight away, or allow them to cool and freeze for future use.

**9.** In the UK, Yorkshire puddings are traditionally served with roast beef , roast potatoes, vegetables, and lashings of gravy. But they are great with any meat dishes or stews.

# Doner Kebab Meat

## Ingredients

500g / 18oz Minced / ground Lamb (20% fat)
2 slices of bread (approx 50g / 2oz)
1 Onion (medium size)
1 Egg (large)
20g Fresh Coriander
20g Fresh flat leaf Parsley
1tsp / 8g Salt
½tsp / 2g Ground black pepper
1tsp / 4g Ground Coriander
1tsp / 4g Ground Paprika (smoked)
1tsp / 4g Ground Chilli powder (Hot)
1tsp / 6 g Garlic granules

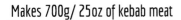

Makes 700g/ 25oz of kebab meat

## Method

**1.** Once all of your ingredients are assembled, preheat you oven to 180°C that's 355°F or gas mark 4.

**2.** Place all of the ingredients apart from the fresh herbs, into a food processor, run your machine for one minute, then add the fresh herbs, and run for a further 30 seconds, you may have to scrape down the sides of the bowl a couple of times, to make sure everything is thoroughly combined.

**3.** Once processed your Doner mix should be a thick smooth paste.

**4.** Turn out your mix onto a piece of greased aluminium foil, and with gloves and oil on your hands, manipulate it into a brick shape, as shown in the image below.

**5.** Close the foil into a tight parcel, place it on a baking tray, and bake in the preheated oven for 50 minutes.

**6.** Allow the meat to rest for 15 minutes before removing the foil.

**7.** When ready, calve very thinly and fill pita breads with it, along with salad and a dressing of your choice.  (See pages 18-19 for Pita bread recipe)

# Perfect Roast Potatoes

## Ingredients

5 Medium size potatoes (Maris Piper, Potatoes Recommended)
100g / 3½oz Goose fat or Beef Dripping
Coarse sea salt, and black pepper, to taste

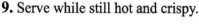

Makes 15 Roast potatoes

## Method

**1.** Wash, peel, and chop each potato into 3 equal pieces.

**2.** Get the washed potatoes into a pan of water, add a ½tsp of salt, and place the pan on a high heat, bring the water to a boil, then turn the heat down to low/medium, and simmer for 6 minutes.

**3.** While the potatoes are simmering, preheat your oven to, 200°C / 390°F.

**4.** Add the Goose fat or Beef Dripping to a roasting pan, and place the roasting pan in the preheated oven, to get the fat good and hot, this should take approx 5 minutes.

**5.** Once the potatoes are boiled, carefully drain them through a colander in your sink, once completely drained, give them a gentle shake in the colander, to roughen up the edges of the hot potatoes.

**6.** Carefully take the hot pan out of the oven, and place it on the top of your stove, and very carefully add the potatoes to the hot fat, turn each potato with a couple of forks to completely coat them in the fat, sprinkle with coarse sea salt and freshly ground black pepper, get them into the hot oven and set your timer for 45 minutes,

**7.** Halfway through the roasting time, carefully give the potatoes a quick turn in the fat for even cooking.

**8.** When the time is up, get these beautiful crispy roast potatoes onto a plate lined with kitchen paper to drain any excess fat, sprinkle with a little more salt and pepper.

**9.** Serve while still hot and crispy.

# Garlic Mushrooms

## Ingredients

4 large flat Mushrooms
4 Cloves of garlic (1 per mushroom)
60g / 4tbls Extra virgin olive oil
¼ of a medium size onion
4g / 1tsp of dried Oregano
10g Fresh basil leaves or 4g /
1 tsp dried basil
4g / ½tsp Salt

Makes 4

Suitable, for Vegan and Vegetarian

## Method

**1.** Before starting the recipe; preheat your oven to 200°C / 390°F / gas mark 6.

**2.** Begin by carefully peeling the skin from the mushrooms, cut the stems from the mushrooms, and set the stems aside for the filling; if you have small stems, you'll need 2 smaller mushrooms to make up the shortfall.

**3.** Place all of the other ingredients into a mini processor including the oil; pulse the machine until the ingredients are chopped small.

**4.** If you don't have a mini processor, use a knife to finely chop all of the dry ingredients, and finally mix with the oil.

**5.** Place the 4 mushrooms on a baking tray and fill each one with the mixture. Don't overfill as they will overflow in the oven.

**6.** Place the tray in the hot oven, and set the timer for 12 minutes.

**7.** After the 12 minutes remove from the oven and serve.

# Crustless Quiche

## Ingredients

5 large eggs
85g / 3oz Mature/strong cheddar cheese, grated
2 Slices of boiled ham
2 Medium spring/green onions
Small bunch of chives
1 Clove garlic
30g / 2tbls Double or single cream
2g / ½tsp Salt
Knob of butter

Serves 2

## Method

**1.** Before starting the recipe, pre heat your oven to 190°C / 375°F / gas mark 5

**2.** Grease a suitable size flan dish or oven proof pan with butter (approx 6in / 15cm)

**3.** Finely chop the onions, garlic,chives, and ham.

**4.** Add the eggs, salt, and cream to a bowl, and whisk for 1 minute,

**5.** Gently fold in the, grated cheese, and the other chopped ingredients, be careful not knock the air out of the mix.

**6.** Transfer the mixture to the buttered dish or pan.

**7.** Carefully place in the preheated oven, and set your timer for 20 minutes.

**8.** After the time is up, remove from the oven and allow it to rest for 2 minutes.

**9.** Carefully remove from the pan/dish and serve hot or cold.

**10.** This quiche goes very well with a red onion salad, and chilli dressing.